English

Philip Allan Updates
Market Place, Deddington, Oxfordshire, OX15 0SE

Orders
Bookpoint Ltd, 130 Milton Park, Abingdon, Oxfordshire, OX14 4SB
tel: (44) 01235 827720
fax: (44) 01235 400454
e-mail: uk.orders@bookpoint.co.uk
Lines are open 9.00 a.m. – 5.00 p.m., Monday to Saturday, with a 24-hour message answering service. You can also order through our website:
www.philipallan.co.uk

© Philip Allan Updates 2006

ISBN-13: 978-1-84489-656-1
ISBN-10: 1-84489-656-0

This guide has been written specifically to support students preparing for AQA(A) GCSE English. The content has been neither approved nor endorsed by AQA and remains the sole responsibility of the author.

Printed in Spain

Environmental information
The paper on which this title is printed is sourced from managed, sustainable forests.

Contents

About this guide

This guide has been written to help you make the most of your skills and achieve the best grade that you can in the assessments for the AQA(A) GCSE English course. You may complete this course over the full 2 years, over four terms, or over 1 year.

It is important that you attempt each part of the course to the best of your ability, even if, for example, you think that you are not as good at speaking and listening as you are at writing.

You can achieve grade A*–G in your coursework assignments, and you will be entered for one of two examination tiers:
▶ higher tier — you can be awarded a grade A*–D (with an extraordinary award at E grade to stop anyone 'falling off' the tier).
▶ foundation tier — you can be awarded a C–G grade.

You will discuss and agree your entry tier with your teacher, but as a general rule:
▶ If your coursework and exam practice work are clearly within the C-grade band of marks, or above, you are a higher-tier candidate.
▶ If your marks are consistently on the C/D boundary, or below, you are a foundation-tier candidate. If you enter for the higher tier, you will miss out on the extra bulleted guidance you are given in Papers 1 and 2, and you may struggle with the difficulty of the reading items.

This guide is divided into sections that each deal with a different aspect of the course. You will need to read all the sections to succeed at your predicted level, but you can read them in the order that you find most useful.

The guide has been designed to be student-friendly and to help you to:
▶ gain an overall view of how and when you will be assessed
▶ clarify what you have been told in class before you begin an assessment

It is *not* meant to undermine or contradict what your teacher tells you. This guide helps you to help yourself and to consolidate your learning.

Hot tip
▶ *Your exam marks count for 60% of your final grade, so it is important that you use this guide to work out exactly what you need to do in each of the exams.*

A fuller picture of the details in this guide can be found in the new GCSE English magazine *Full English*, published by Philip Allan Updates and edited by the author of this guide.

Assessment overview

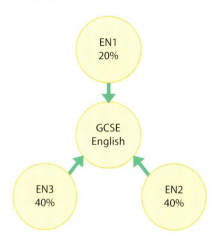

Speaking and listening (EN1) — you will be assessed on three pieces of speaking and listening as part of your coursework. This counts for 20% of your final grade.

Reading (EN2) — you will be assessed on four pieces of reading: two in coursework and two in the examinations. The coursework pieces count for 10% and the examination pieces count for 30% of your final grade.

Writing (EN3) — again, there are four pieces of assessment: two in coursework and two in the examinations. The coursework pieces count for 10% and the exam pieces count for 30% of your final grade.

Hot tip

▶ If you can talk about something in your own words, it means that you can understand it.

Hot tip

▶ There are three times more marks available for the exam pieces than for the coursework, but both require the same skills. Coursework allows you to practise these skills before the exams.

Coursework

Overview

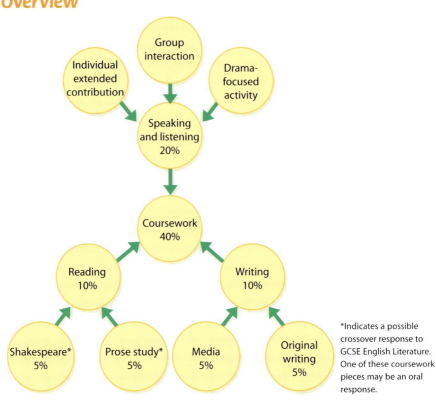

*Indicates a possible crossover response to GCSE English Literature. One of these coursework pieces may be an oral response.

Q and A

Q: Why aren't there more marks available for speaking and listening?

A: *The mark allocation is the same for all examination boards — this has been standardised by the government.*

Q: Can I use the internet to download other students' work to help me with my coursework?

Hot tip

▶ To get the grade you deserve, you must attempt all pieces of coursework. You must also attempt every part of every question in each exam. If you fail to attempt a question, your final grade will suffer.

A: *You must be careful not to cheat, otherwise you may put all your GCSE grades at risk. The regulations state that:*

▶ *The work you submit must be your own.*

▶ *You must not copy the words and ideas of someone else or allow another candidate to copy from you.*

▶ *You must show your sources and a bibliography.*

If you are in any doubt, ask your teacher.

Q: How many pieces of work can I do on the computer?

A: *Only one piece of work has to be in your own handwriting.*

Q: Do I have to write about my prose text/Shakespeare play, or can I talk about it with my teacher instead?

A: *You can submit one of your EN2 responses orally, as long as you also submit a brief written description of your work.*

Q: How long do my pieces of coursework have to be?

A: *Two to three sides of A4 is plenty. You are not marked on how many words you write — you get marked on the skills you show. The exam papers are marked in the same way, so you should use your coursework to develop the reading and writing skills that you will need to demonstrate in the exams.*

Q: How is studying Shakespeare at GCSE different from studying it at Key Stage 3?

A: *You have more scope to choose your own activities at GCSE. You will be able to discuss the different options for tasks with your teacher. One popular task is to focus on a particular scene and then to film or direct it. You can also use this as preparation for the EN1 drama-focused activity and the EN3 original writing and media tasks.*

Q: When will I be assessed?

A: *Coursework is assessed throughout the course, as and when appropriate. Your teacher will give you a specific timetable for each piece of reading and writing coursework and will tell you when you are expected to deliver your EN1 assessments.*

Coursework assignments

You will probably submit four written pieces of coursework for English: prose study, Shakespeare, original writing and media. You may complete more than four, but you will decide with your teacher which are the best ones to submit. If you have submitted a fifth piece of coursework, this will probably be assessed for English Literature only (post-1914 drama).

Reading (prose study)

Most students submit a combined English/Literature folder, so your prose study assignment will be based on a text:
- ▶ published before 1914 (students submitting a folder for English alone may choose a text from the post-1914 period)
- ▶ by an author on the National Curriculum list (see p. 68 of the specification, or ask your teacher)
- ▶ which is 'substantial' — a novel or a collection of five or six short stories by the same or different authors

Hints

- ▶ Remember that it is the quality, not the quantity, of your work that counts. You must focus your comments on showing that you understand:
  - – what the novel/short story is about
  - – the style, structure and characterisation of the novel/short story
  - – why the writer chose to write in the way that he/she did
  - – how the writer uses language and form for effect
  - – when and where the novel/short story is set

Your teacher will mark your work based on your understanding of the above points — simply retelling the story will not gain you many marks.
- ▶ You must use quotations or references to back up your arguments in a reading assessment. Remember to **PEE** — point, example, explain.
- ▶ If you are writing a crossover piece, you should mention the social, cultural or historical background of the text.

Reading (Shakespeare)

You will probably include this as a crossover piece with English Literature.

Although you may have already studied some Shakespeare at Key Stage 3, you will find that you have more freedom at GCSE to:
- ▶ analyse — work out what you think a scene or character is about
- ▶ interpret — make sense of what you have been asked to do
- ▶ evaluate — weigh up your views against those of others

You should try to use these skills in your work, as they are what examiners are looking for when deciding whether to award an A grade.

Hints

- ▶ The hints from the previous section (prose study) are also relevant to your Shakespeare coursework.
- ▶ When you are studying Shakespeare, remember that you are reading a

play that is meant to be performed on stage. Try to think about the effectiveness of what you are reading as a play.

▶ Try to appreciate the play from the standpoint of a young person in the twenty-first century.

▶ The issues that Shakespeare deals with are still important today. Think about how well Shakespeare handles subjects such as racism, war, nationalism, love, family and mysticism.

▶ Imagine how you would update a Shakespeare play for a modern audience. You could watch Baz Luhrmann's version of *Romeo and Juliet* to give you some ideas.

▶ Remember that one of your reading pieces of coursework can be presented orally. You could use a computer program such as PowerPoint to present your work.

TOPFOTO

Writing (original writing)

In this piece of coursework, you are writing to imagine, explore and entertain. Many students enjoy writing this piece of coursework most. You should look upon this coursework as practice for the two pieces of writing that you will have to produce in the examinations, so you should aim to write between two and three sides of A4. However, it is the quality of your work that counts, not the quantity.

All GCSE English writing is assessed using the same rules (skills descriptors), so you should go through the same process whenever you write:

▶ Read the question.
▶ Brainstorm a range of ideas.
▶ Plan the shape of your piece.
▶ Write your piece.
▶ Check your piece for mistakes.

Hints

▶ You should:
  – engage the interest of the reader
  – use the shape and structure of your writing effectively
  – focus on controlling sentence variety for effect

- choose appropriate words to use
- be original

▶ Use the writing of others to give you ideas for your own work:
- Look at the way your pre-1914 novelist sets a scene.
- Notice how films and television dramas are structured.
- Begin to build up a wide vocabulary by listening and reading.
- Pay attention to song lyrics for imaginative uses of words.
- Start a 'sketch book' in which you collect ideas from others and begin to develop a creative voice of your own.

▶ Think carefully about the purpose and audience of your piece of writing. Although the only person to read it will probably be your English teacher and your purpose will be to reach your target grade, think beyond this and try to display the full range of your writing skills.

Writing (media)

In this piece of coursework, you are writing to analyse, review and comment. You should not see this as a piece of media studies coursework, but as a piece of English written coursework based on your reading of media. Although most students eventually choose to complete coursework based on the moving image (film, television etc.), it is better if you complete three pieces on:

▶ moving images
▶ newspapers and magazines
▶ advertisements

This will give you a number of pieces from which to choose for your submission at the end of the course. It will also help you to prepare for the media reading question on Paper 1.

Hot tip

▶ Remember that this piece of coursework makes up only 5% of your final grade, and the reading of media question on Paper 1 is worth approximately 7.5% (approximately half of the 15% available for reading questions in Paper 1).

Hints

▶ Remember to refer to the writing skills for this piece of work. Although it is based on your reading, it is your writing that is assessed.
▶ If you write about something you are familiar with, and are enthusiastic about, you are more likely to engage the reader's interest (this is one of the main descriptors for GCSE writing). You may choose to write about:

- a series of television adverts
- MTV videos
- the internet
- a particular type of magazine
- a film genre, e.g. horror or fantasy
- a soap opera

▶ You may know more about your chosen medium than your teacher, so this piece of coursework is a good place to display your knowledge of:
- interesting aspects of this medium
- different organisational devices
- technical vocabulary on this subject (especially films and the internet)
- interesting presentational devices

Speaking and listening

Speaking and listening are worth 20% of your overall English mark so they are important components of the course. Speaking and listening form the basis of your learning throughout the 2-year GCSE course — if you are able to speak about something in your own words, it means that you understand it.

There are three units of work (triplets) on which you will be assessed. You must use speech to:
▶ explain, describe, narrate
▶ explore, analyse, imagine
▶ discuss, argue, persuade

There are also three assessment objectives against which you will be marked. You will be expected to:
▶ communicate clearly
▶ take part in discussion
▶ adopt roles

Finally, there are three contexts within which you will be assessed:
▶ individual extended contribution
▶ group discussion
▶ drama-focused activities

Your English teacher may choose to link these with other aspects of the course, or may choose to set up three specific sessions within which to assess your performance. For example, you may be asked to take part in a group discussion on poems from the *Anthology*, where you explore the meanings, analyse the techniques and imagine possible links with other

poems. On the other hand, your teacher may assess your general ability to take part in group discussions and will choose for your submission the situation in which you achieved most from throughout the 2-year course.

The following sections look at the three contexts in more detail.

Individual extended contribution

You have a considerable amount of flexibility with this part of your course-work. It can take place over a number of sessions and your teacher can choose to mark you against any of the three triplets.

To fulfil the assessment objectives for this activity, you must:
▶ speak clearly and try to interest your audience
▶ structure your contribution so that your audience knows what you are trying to say
▶ speak at some length
▶ use appropriate language for the situation, e.g. standard English

Possible tasks include:
▶ a talk on a subject area of interest
▶ an explanation of a game, process etc.
▶ a film review using a PowerPoint presentation
▶ reporting back on group work to the class
▶ a main speech in a debate

Hot tips
▶ *Don't simply read your speech from a script, but do use brief notes or bullet points.*
▶ *Ask your teacher for guidance on how to use your notes.*
▶ *Don't over-rehearse your talk or learn it by heart — this will not engage your audience.*
▶ *If talking in front of a large audience worries you, you can talk in front of a smaller group of sympathetic friends.*
▶ *Ask your teacher if you can deliver your contribution based on a recent event that interested you — for example, work experience, a holiday.*
▶ *This is an extended contribution, so enjoy the time and scope.*

Group discussion

When you work as part of a group, it is important that you concentrate on engaging in discussion with others — this is not the time for showing off with a solo performance.

Although your group can have as few as two people, it will be difficult to access the higher mark bands in such a small group. You will find it hard to show that you can chair a group discussion and help others to contribute. It is therefore better to work in a larger group. The best groups have a mixture of personalities, abilities and opinions — working in friendship groups is rarely the best way to approach this task.

The group skills that you need in this part of your coursework will be important to you in later life. In the workplace, you have to interact with others, debate, negotiate and come to a resolution — you should see this part of your coursework as an opportunity to develop these skills.

To fulfil the assessment objectives for this activity, you must:
▶ take an active part in the discussion
▶ speak and listen
▶ evaluate the contributions of others and the reasons for their contributions
▶ evaluate the roles of others in the group
▶ encourage others to contribute

Possible tasks include:
▶ a discussion of poems, in which you can explore, analyse and imagine
▶ solving a problem by exploring different opinions and points of view, demonstrating that you can discuss, argue and persuade
▶ a discussion of a controversial issue, in which you can explain, describe and narrate

Hot tips

▶ *You must listen to other members of the group and engage with them and the purpose of the task.*
▶ *There is a clear progression through the grade boundaries, from making some contribution, to a clear and sustained engagement, to initiating and developing discussion.*
▶ *Remember that the skills you use as a reader are similar to those you use as a speaker and listener.*

Drama-focused activities

In this activity, you will probably work as part of a group, and your piece may be either improvised or prepared. Unlike in the previous two contexts, you must adopt a role or play a part for this piece of coursework. Whatever you choose to do, you will be assessed mainly on how well you project your role or character.

Many drama-focused activities take the form of simulations or the hot-seating of characters. If you choose to carry out a different piece of work for your drama-focused activity, your teacher may still set you a hot-seating or simulation task, as this can be used for your contribution to group interaction.

To fulfil the assessment objectives for this activity, you must:
► adopt a role
► communicate with the audience
► use a range of dramatic techniques

Possible tasks include:
► exploring an issue from different roles and points of view — for example, the issue of teenagers roaming an estate from the viewpoint of teenagers, parents and the police
► role playing within simulations is popular because there is a lot of material available to help you prepare
► using your pre- and post-1914 drama texts as a springboard for developing additional scenes or adapting a situation for modern audiences

Hot tips

► *In this activity, the grade progression is from adopting a simple role, to being able to engage with the audience, to being able to create a complex role using a range of techniques, to controlling the audience's response.*
► *Wearing just one item of costume (a hat, jacket or pair of glasses) can help you to adopt a role and maintain it.*
► *It is not only about what, or how much, you say — it is also about your engagement with the task and your body language.*

Examinations

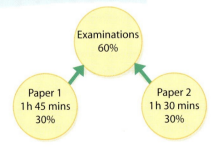

Examinations
60%

Paper 1
1 h 45 mins
30%

Paper 2
1 h 30 mins
30%

Paper 1

- ▶ Section A requires reading responses to unseen non-fiction and media texts:
  - – There will be two or more passages/items.
  - – At least one passage will be assessed for media.
- ▶ Section B requires writing to argue, persuade or advise — this may be linked to the theme of Section A.
- ▶ You are advised to spend 1 hour on Section A and 45 minutes on Section B.

Paper 2

- ▶ Section A requires a reading response to poetry from the different cultures section of the AQA *Anthology*.
- ▶ Section B requires writing to inform, explain or describe.
- ▶ You are advised to spend 45 minutes on each section.

Paper 1 reading

Q and A

Q: Can I answer the reading questions on Paper 1 in bullet point form?

A: *No. The instructions on the front of the exam paper state that candidates should answer the questions 'in continuous prose'. This means that you should write in full sentences. It is useful to structure your answers with words and phrases such as 'first', 'the author then goes on to…', 'next…' etc.*

Q: Why do I have to read 'two or more passages' in the exam paper?

A: *One passage must be in continuous prose to support a question on following an argument. Another passage must have interesting organisational, presentational or linguistic devices about which you can answer a media question.*

Q: How long should I spend on each question in Section A?

A: *You should double the total marks available for each question (8 × 2 = 16) and spend this number of minutes on each question. It is especially important not to spend too long on the first question, to avoid running out of time later on.*

Q: Does it matter if I miss out a question?

A: *Yes. It is hard to gain full marks for a question, but it is easy to attempt a question and gain at least some marks.*

Q: What is the best way to prepare for the reading on Paper 1?

A: *You should read as many types of non-fiction as possible (e.g. newspaper and magazine articles, adverts, web pages, leaflets, fliers, biographies). You should also familiarise yourself with the assessment objectives for this paper.*

Q: Where will I be asked about media texts and what are they?

A: *Media texts are means of communication that reach large numbers of people, such as advertisements, film, newspapers or television. You will be asked about media texts in Question 2 on Paper 1. The question(s) cover presentational, organisational and linguistic devices, which are related to assessment objective EN2(v).*

EN2 **assessment objectives**

This section explains each of the five Paper 1 EN2 assessment objectives in turn. Guidance is given on what is required to gain the three key grades of F, C and A, and example A-grade answers (based on the 'Think! Don't Drink and Drive' leaflet on p. 15) are included. The answers were written in response to a general question about the structure of the leaflet and the devices used by the writer.

EN2(i)

Read in detail and with interest, expressing your own opinion and backing it up with the PEE (point, example, explanation) structure.

Grade F	The student attempts to answer the question but copies a lot of the original text.
Grade C	The student clearly tries to answer the question and to structure his/her answer.
Grade A	The student gives a full answer, showing that he/she has understood the passage fully and can shape and absorb.

It is my opinion that this leaflet is against any drink driving at all. There are several sections of the leaflet that would support this view apart from the main heading on the front. The first panel on the inside of the leaflet suggests that even the smallest amount of alcohol can affect your driving performance and lists the effects and the factors that determine how alcohol will make you act differently.

Hot tip

▶ *This answer is a good example of what **shaping** and **absorbing** actually mean.*

Drink driving and the law

If you are convicted of:	The maximum penalty is:
Causing death by careless driving when under the influence of drink or drugs	14 years' imprisonment, an unlimited fine, disqualification from driving for at least 2 years and a mandatory extended driving test
Driving or attempting to drive whilst above the legal limit or unfit through drink	6 months' imprisonment, a fine of up to £5,000 and disqualification from driving for at least 12 months' (3 years if convicted twice in 10 years)
Being in charge of a vehicle whilst above the legal limit or unfit through drink	3 months' imprisonment, a fine of up to £2,500 and discretionary disqualification from driving
Refusing to provide a specimen of breath, blood or urine for analysis	6 months' imprisonment, a fine of up to £5,000 and disqualification from driving for at least 12 months

Further copies of this leaflet can be obtained from DfT Free Literature on 0870 1226 236.

Published by the Department for Transport.
© Crown copyright November 2005.
Paper comprising at least 75% recycled fibre. Prod code TINF002.

THINK!
Don't Drink and Drive
www.thinkroadsafety.gov.uk

When will you have had too much?

THINK!
Don't Drink and Drive

You can't calculate your alcohol limit, so don't try.

Any amount of alcohol affects your ability to drive safely. The effects can include:

- slower reactions
- increased stopping distance
- poorer judgement of speed and distance
- reduced field of vision

Alcohol also tends to make you feel over-confident and more likely to take risks when driving, which increases the danger to all road users, including yourself.

If you drive at twice the current legal alcohol limit* you are at least 50 times more likely to be involved in a fatal car crash compared to a driver who has not been drinking.

There is no failsafe guide as to how to stay under the legal alcohol limit or how much you can drink and still drive safely.

It depends on:

- your weight, sex, age, metabolism
- stress levels
- an empty stomach
- the amount and type of alcohol

The only safe option is not to drink if you plan to drive. Never offer a drink to someone else who is driving.

*The legal alcohol limit for driving in the UK is 80 milligrammes of alcohol in 100 millilitres of blood.

Drinking and driving don't mix

3,000 people are killed or seriously injured on our roads each year in drink drive related crashes and nearly one in six of all deaths on the road involve drivers who are over the legal limit. If you plan to drink, don't risk driving:

- book a taxi
- use public transport
- stay overnight
- arrange for someone who is not drinking to drive
- don't be tempted to get into a car with anyone else who has been drinking.

Consequences of drink driving

If you think you won't get caught, you're wrong. Around 100,000 drivers are convicted every year for drink driving. You don't have to be in a crash to be breath tested. The police can ask you to take a breath test if they suspect you have been drinking, or if you commit a traffic offence. If you're convicted of drink driving:

- you'll have a criminal record
- you won't be allowed to drive for at least a year
- you could lose your job
- your lifestyle could change dramatically
- you will have higher insurance costs
- your driving licence will be endorsed for 11 years
- during that time you will find it difficult to hire a car or get a job if you are, or hope to become, a professional driver

The morning after

If you've been out drinking you may still be affected by alcohol the next day. Even though you may feel OK when you get up, you may be over the legal alcohol limit or unfit to drive, and could still lose your licence. It's impossible to get rid of alcohol any faster. A shower, cup of coffee, or other ways of 'sobering up' will not help. It just takes time.

There are no excuses

"I had a drink but it was at lunch time"
Even a small drink at lunchtime can make you more sleepy and impair your driving.

"I feel fine to drive"
Any amount of alcohol will affect your judgement.

"I've only had a couple"
Even a single drink will affect your driving performance.

"I've had a meal"
Alcohol just takes a little longer to get into your system, your driving will still be affected.

"I can handle my drink"
You may think you can handle your drink, but you will have difficulty judging distance and speed. Your reactions are slower, so it will take you longer to stop.

"I'm only going down the road"
A large proportion of all drink drive crashes occur within 3 miles of the start of the journey.

"I'm driving slowly and carefully"
Alcohol actually makes you less alert.

EN2(ii)

Tell the difference between fact and opinion and work out how something is laid out on the page.

Grade F	The student makes a general comment about facts and opinions and describes how something looks on the page.
Grade C	The student identifies, understands and comments on both the use of facts and opinions and how text is presented.
Grade A	The student makes clear judgements, possibly giving a variety of views, and weighs up the ways in which text is presented.

There are many facts and opinions in this leaflet, but I am going to focus on the uses of one of each. On the back page of the leaflet it states that the maximum penalty for causing death by careless driving is 14 years' imprisonment. This is the first point of law mentioned because the writer wants it to have the maximum effect. This leaflet is mainly made up of facts because it wants to educate and warn, but it is the opinion of this leaflet that, as you cannot calculate the effect of alcohol, you should not drive after drinking, for example where it says: 'The only safe option is not to drink.' This is the opinion of this leaflet, and it does not fit in with the current UK law. Although this is a laudable stance, and is used for beneficial reasons to prevent accidents, it is clearly the opinion of the Department of Transport, and it may be used as a political position to influence law makers.

Hot tip

▶ It is not the length of your answer that counts, it is the quality and detail — you must give examples and explain them.

EN2(iii)

Work out what a writer is talking about and understand how what he/she says can have more than one meaning.

Grade F	The student tends to tell the story and to misunderstand some of what the writer is saying.
Grade C	The student makes a clear attempt to work out what the writer is saying within some sort of structure.
Grade A	The student gives a complete, detailed answer covering all parts of the question and passage.

The writer of this leaflet gives several reasons for his/her wholehearted argument that drivers should not drink at all if they are driving. First, the leaflet stresses the dangers of driving after drinking alcohol and lists alternatives, because the writer is not against drinking: just drink driving. Then the writer spells out what would happen if you were caught drink driving. Additionally, the writer argues against the stock excuses and 'old wives' tales' that most people give for continuing to drink and drive, despite the evidence. Finally, the main argument of the leaflet is that you cannot work out your alcohol limit because there are too many variables.

Hot tip

▶ *This student has not written a lot but has covered all parts of the leaflet in plenty of detail. Remember that you do not necessarily have to write a lot of words to produce an A-grade answer.*

EN2(iv)

Use parts of the text to support your points (from different texts if appropriate) and compare different texts.

Grade F	The student tends to refer to parts of texts and to write about two or more texts separately without really comparing them.
Grade C	The student clearly uses the PEE structure and can find 'chunks' of text to support his/her point of view.
Grade A	The student is able to find just the right reference or quotation or to put it in his/her own words if required and to make a detailed comparison between texts.

This leaflet takes a hard line on drinking and driving, delivering a very strong message that it is wrong under any circumstances, even down to the fact that you can still be unfit to drive the morning after having had a drink, for example where it states you 'could still lose your licence'. **This is very different** from the drinking in moderation and the unit-driven message that is usually given to students in PSE lessons. It also differs from the sort of message that the Licensed Victuallers Association would give. **However, it is similar** to the message that police forces nationwide give in their drink drive campaigns in the run up to Christmas, which is **nearly always something like** 'Think! Don't Drink and Drive'.

Hot tip

▶ You should use comparison words, such as those highlighted in red on p. 17, to provide evidence that you can compare different texts.

EN2(v)

Work out and put a value on how writers use different devices to make their work look good on the page and to use words for effect.

Grade F	The student tends to identify devices or make general points about any devices that the writer may use.
Grade C	The student can make a clear point about how writers use words for effect and can select examples of each.
Grade A	The student can put a value on the different devices used by writers for specific reasons.

The most striking presentational device is the image of a beer glass on the front of the leaflet, with different levels marked on the side of the glass to suggest that it is impossible to measure when an individual has had too much to drink. **This works really well because the meaning of the image is not immediately clear. However, when the penny drops, the reader understands the significance of the dirty 'tide-marks' on the glass.** The writer has chosen to use subheadings in yellow against black to organise the leaflet. **This is clever because it reflects the sorts of colours used by the police when cordoning off an accident or other incident, so it acts as a visual warning as well as an organisational aid.** Finally, the main thing you notice when reading this leaflet is the restricted semantic field regarding personal pronouns. The writer addresses the reader in the second person much of the time, for example 'you'll have a criminal record'. In the final sub-heading, the writer uses the first person, where the statement and answer format **almost reflects the sorts of things a guilty driver would say to a policeman on being breathalysed, which works well as a deterrent.**

Hot tip

▶ The best way to prepare for this part of the exam is to read as many different types of non-fiction as possible, from the back of your cereal packet to biographies. The writing highlighted in red above shows where the candidate has fulfilled A-grade requirements by evaluating the devices used by the writer.

Paper 2 reading

Q and A

Q: I have read all the poems from the second cluster. How many questions can I answer in the exam?

A: *The first question will always be set on poems from Cluster 1 and the second from Cluster 2, so you will be able to answer only one question.*

Q: What is the question going to be next summer?

A: *Obviously, only the Senior Examiners know this, but the question will ask you to make comparisons. The named poem is unlikely to have been set before on this exam paper.*

Q: My sister took her own *Anthology* into the exam, in which she had written notes. Why can't I do that?

A: *From summer 2005, the government changed the rules so that all students must be given a clean Anthology in the exam. This ensures that everybody is treated the same. Examiners were finding it difficult to decide what mark to award those students who had simply copied out the notes they had written around the poems. It also means that you are more likely to focus on answering the question that has actually been set, rather than simply copying out your notes.*

Q: Should I write a plan?

A: *Yes. If you write a plan, you are more likely to focus on answering the question on the exam paper. You are therefore more likely to fulfil the assessment objectives.*

Q: What is the best way to revise for this exam?

A: *The best way to revise is to reread the poems in a different order — don't always begin with the first poem and work your way through to the end. In addition, try to read the poems with the three assessment objectives in mind: what you think the poems mean; how the poet uses devices to make this meaning clear; and how the poems are similar and different.*

Q: What is the difference between the foundation- and higher-tier questions?

A: *Foundation-tier questions are designed to give you more guidance and structure before you start writing. Foundation-tier questions always have bullet points that give you a way into the questions and to help you to show what you know and appreciate about the poems.*

Q: What is the best way to answer a question?

A: *The flow diagram below shows a successful method of answering questions for this exam.*

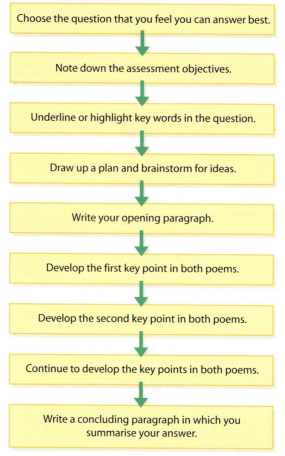

Choose the question that you feel you can answer best.

Note down the assessment objectives.

Underline or highlight key words in the question.

Draw up a plan and brainstorm for ideas.

Write your opening paragraph.

Develop the first key point in both poems.

Develop the second key point in both poems.

Continue to develop the key points in both poems.

Write a concluding paragraph in which you summarise your answer.

Brainstorming is best done within a chart such as the one below. You can draw a chart on one page of your answer booklet. You should spend approximately 10 minutes on creating your plan.

	Named poem from question	**Your choice of poem**
Ideas, feelings attitudes	This is similar to…	However…
Devices used by the poets	Both poets…	On the other hand…
Cultures and personal view	The two poems are similar because…	but…

EN2 *assessment objectives*

This section explains each of the Paper 2 EN2 assessment objectives in turn. There are three assessment objectives for this paper — each one is worth a third of the available marks for each question.

This section also gives guidance on what is required to gain the three key grades of F, C and A, and includes examples of A-grade answers. The answers provided were written in response to a general question comparing what two different poets have to say about different cultures. The poems used as examples are 'Unrelated Incidents' and 'Half-Caste' from Cluster 2.

EN2(i)

Read in detail and with interest, expressing your own opinion and backing it up with the PEE (point, example, explanation) structure.

Grade F	The student tends to make simple comments supported by some sort of reference.
Grade C	The student shows a clear understanding of feelings, attitudes and ideas.
Grade A	The student begins to explore his/her own ideas and can show appreciation of the ideas expressed by the poet.

Both poets have similar but different views about the cultures they are writing about and represent. Leonard seems to be very annoyed that anyone would be narrow-minded enough to judge anyone else by the way they speak. He says: 'wanna yoo scruff' to get his point across in a very blunt manner. This will be particularly meaningful to many teenagers who are continually being judged by the way they speak and dress. This is similar to the views expressed by Agard, who begins his poem in a very accusatory fashion by stating: 'Excuse me' and goading

the person addressed in the poem continually to support their point of view about judging people by halves instead of judging the whole person.

The reader can't help thinking that both poets are really addressing the public at large and that each poet is making a more general point about institutionalised prejudice.

Hot tip

▶ Notice how this student has begun to explore his/her own ideas as well as starting to show detailed understanding of the poet's ideas. This is what you should aim for in your responses.

EN2(ii)

Select the right quotation for the point you want to prove and use material from two poems to compare.

Grade F	The student can refer to at least some detail to help to explain his/her point.
Grade C	The student makes effective use of quotation and comparisons.
Grade A	The student's references and points are hard to tell apart — they are integrated.

Leonard especially shows his disdain for anyone who would be so small-minded as to value one person's 'trooth' more than someone else's by the way they speak. By repeating the word 'scruff', and using the vernacular continually in lines like 'yooz doant no' he goads the reader (especially a literate reader like an English teacher!) into some sort of response. Agard uses the same device of repetition by beginning each of his taunts with the same construction. He asks the reader directly to explain their racist point of view by chanting 'wha yu mean'. The very lack of formality of this phrase has exactly the same effect as Leonard's. However, Agard's poem is a sort of dialogue between the narrator and his audience who is belittled every bit as much as Leonard makes a fool of his imaginary audience.

EN2(iii)

Understand and appreciate how writers use linguistic, structural and presentational devices to help them get their message across.

Grade F	The student makes some sort of statement on some devices.
Grade C	The student makes a clear attempt to explain how writers link techniques and purpose.
Grade A	The student makes a close and detailed explanation of the writer's techniques.

Each of the poets uses different techniques in order to make their message clearer: Leonard does not use any literary devices such as similes or alliteration because that would weaken the main point of his poem — that you do not need to use standard English or standard poetic devices. He relies more heavily on the narrow shape and phonetic spelling of the poem to make an effect on the reader. Agard uses rhyme in several lines, for example 44 and 46, to accentuate the meaning of the rhymed words and to add to the performance nature of his poem. You could hardly call this poem conventional, but the poem does have an organisation by dint of the poet's use of stanzas as well as the already mentioned repetition. What is striking about both poems is that each poet has tried to think of a novel way of presenting the poem to the reader in order to accentuate the meaning.

For that reason, I believe that these two poets are eminently successful in sharing their views about the general public's ignorance about the effects of cultural 'blindness' on large groups of people.

Hot tip

▶ You should remind yourself of the three assessment objectives before you start to plan your answer. This will ensure that you fulfil them throughout your response, as this candidate does.

Papers 1 and 2 writing

Q and A

Q: Should I write a plan?

A: *Yes. A plan will help you to fulfil the assessment objectives. The examiner wants you to engage his/her interest; to write within a structure; to use*

sentences and words for effect and to write with some technical accuracy. Your plan should help you to do this by listing some of the interesting, relevant points that you want to make. After having put these into a suitable sequence, you will have already addressed two of the main points that the examiner will be looking for. While you are making your plan, you should also think about the various sentence types, structures and devices that you intend to use.

Q: If I do write a plan, does it get marked?

A: *No. However, it is vitally important that you make a plan, as it will underpin everything that you will write in your answer.*

Q: Which question should I choose on each paper if I want to get a C grade or above?

A: *There are four questions on each paper — argue, persuade and advise on Paper 1 and inform, explain and describe on Paper 2, plus one question on each paper linking two of the types. Your choice should depend on whether you think that you will be able to engage the interest of the examiner. To be able to make an informed choice, you should be aware of the types of writing required and how they are similar and different.*

Q: How much should I write?

A: *You should aim to write about two sides of normal-sized handwriting. However, it is perfectly possible to gain full marks from one and a half sides if you show evidence of the A* descriptors. It is not the quantity of words that counts, it is the quality and the skills that you show. You can do this only with proper planning and preparation.*

Q: How much time should I spend on planning, and how much time on writing my answer?

A: *You should use your 45 minutes productively:*

▶ *Read the question and underline key words — 2 minutes.*
▶ *Plan your writing and where you will show specific skills — 8 minutes.*
▶ *Write your answer, referring back to your plan regularly — 30 minutes.*
▶ *Check for accuracy and fluency — 5 minutes.*

EN3 *assessment objectives*

This section explains the three EN3 assessment objectives, using language similar to that found in the specification. This section also gives an example of an A-grade answer for each type of writing. Although there are far more similarities than differences between the six forms of writing, students who are aiming for a D grade or above should be able to recognise some of the differences.

To fulfil the assessment objectives, you must be able to:

(i) write clearly and imaginatively, and be able to adapt the different forms of writing for different purposes and audiences

(ii) organise your work into sentences, paragraphs and whole pieces of writing using a variety of linguistic and structural features

(iii) use a range of sentence structures effectively with accurate punctuation and spelling

Paper 1
Question 3: writing to argue
When writing to argue, you should:
▶ express your own point of view about a subject
▶ be aware that there are other points of view
▶ make generalised points rather than simply writing in the first person

Should exams be banned?

In the following article I am going to argue that all examinations should be banned and that students should be awarded grades according to their first names, their postcodes and the neatness of their handwriting. I am, of course, joking. However, I am going to argue that examinations play far too important a role in the lives of young people in the UK today.

Employers complain continually that examination grades are of little or no use when choosing between candidates for a job. On the other hand, they are the first to try to head-hunt graduates from the best universities. It is my opinion that there are important things to learn from examination results, but that employers need to give more specialised tests to identify the skills that candidates may need. Would you employ someone for a job in a call centre without first testing their telephone manner? I think not, so examination results should be seen as only one indicator.

Hot tip
▶ *This candidate has engaged the interest of the reader with humour, made generalised points, used a wide vocabulary and obviously had an overall structure in mind. The rest of this article had some presentational devices typical of those found in newspaper articles, such as bullet points and text boxes with captions. However, the candidate has not wasted time by including too many presentational devices and has concentrated on the quality of the article's content.*

Question 4: writing to persuade

When writing to persuade, you should:

▶ try to make someone do or think something that they might not normally consider
▶ make several points to persuade the reader
▶ use different ways to persuade, such as rhetorical devices and second-guessing

27 Trevor Road
Bearstown
Clanarshire
PL6 7TS
8 September 2006

The Angling Globe
The Heronry
Talbut Square
London
SW3 5TF

Dear Editor,

As a regular contributor to your letters page, I would like to try to persuade your readers to visit the northwest of England to sample the many different types of fishing available. How could you spend the rest of your life knowing that there is a region of the country with such a vast array of fishing venues? From sea to canal and from fly to ledger, this is the only region to offer so much variety of fishing as well as variety of settings. How long will it be until you visit?

Picture yourself fishing by the side of a majestic lake with the fells towering over you. Next day you could be standing waist deep in a raging torrent while you try to outwit a large salmon. This region needs someone with your breadth of ability and courage to make the most of what's on offer…

Hot tip

▶ *This candidate has appealed directly to the reader and has used rhetorical questions and the second person to include the reader. As the question asked candidates to write a letter, the candidate has laid out his/her work in the most appropriate manner.*

Question 5: writing to advise

When writing to advise, you should:

► make sure that you write for the audience specified in the question

► write directly to the audience in a persuasive way

► try to come across as someone who knows some, if not all, of the answers

So you want to change your bedroom into a crash-pad for a sophisti-cated young adult who likes to spend a bit of time alone, as well as entertaining friends and keeping in touch via the web. If you want your room to look both pricey and pimpin'; if you want your friends to be both jealous and jumpin'; if you want your parents to be both included and excluded — you've come to the right person for advice. Cleo Tattinger, the presenter of *Pimp my Bedroom*, is here to give you advice on how to gain maximum effect with minimum outlay.

Let's start with the most important aspect of this whole project: the cost (which invariably means the aged parents!) My first piece of advice is to sit down and write a list of reasons why this is bound to be such a good idea for everyone in the household. Your parents will be impressed with your new-found maturity and this new study-centre that you are planning: don't mention the word 'pimpin'', because they may not understand. How about something like *Changing Rooms*? More Llewellyn-Bowen than Tattinger will put their minds at rest.

Question 6

This question focuses on two of the types of writing linked together (e.g. argue and persuade). Whichever types of writing you are asked to use, your answer should concentrate on purpose, audience, structure, sentences, vocabulary choice and accuracy.

Paper 2

Question 3: writing to inform

When writing to inform, you should:

► tell your audience something interesting

► use discourse markers to make sure that your writing is logical and fluent

► remember that sophisticated vocabulary, variety of sentences and structure are important with this form of writing

Hot tip

▶ There is usually no specified audience or genre in Paper 2, so you can write for a real audience (teacher or examiner) and a real purpose (to show the required skills for a C grade or above).

So you want to find out more about my hobby? So you think philately is boring? So who says philately will get you nowhere? My stamp collection has got me into numerous magazines and has led to me meeting a lot of very interesting people from all over the world. Why? Because I was lucky enough to inherit my grandad's stamp collection that he told nobody about, but contained many of the most precious stamps of the early twentieth century.

My collection is insured for over £500,000: now are you interested? In addition, one stamp alone could buy two of the houses in my street. Consequently, I keep very quiet about my collection. I suppose you too will keep quiet about it if I inform you about my collection and tell you how to begin a collection for a young person that you may know. Interested now? Well, let's start at the beginning…

I am lucky in that both of my grandparents are alive, but I am going to explain why my grandad is so important to me. I could say something meaningless, like 'my grandad is always there for me', but that would be a gross simplification of what he has done for me in my 16 years.

To begin with, he is the father of my mum and without her, I would not be here now. But it is his relationship with me that I wish to explain. He is important to me for several reasons, but first and foremost he listens to me when I need someone to talk to. Being a teacher, you will understand how important it is for teenagers to have someone to share their thoughts and problems with. My grandad has listened to my juvenile gurglings since my first utterances on the day of my birth. Even then he could always understand what I was going on about and has continued to do so up until this date.

Question 5: writing to describe

When writing to describe, you should:
▶ try to make the description come to life
▶ produce an interesting opening and an appropriate ending
▶ try to be original and adventurous in your choice of words and sentences

The town centre sleeps. Its main roads lie like limbs spreading from the torso which has the Town Hall at its heart and the Library at the head of the Main Street. The only movement is the slow and regular flashing of the lights by the zebra crossing and the slow crawling of lorries making their way from the local distribution centre.

The town centre sleeps. The shops are all closed apart from the newsagent's, which is taking delivery of its papers and will soon be lively with delivery boys on bikes and skateboards. Right now the only movement is from the owner who is stacking and packing while chatting to the odd early customer passing on the way to work.

The town centre sleeps, but it is beginning to awaken as cars begin to roar around the various corners and head towards the main arteries…

Question 6

This question focuses on two of the types of writing linked together (e.g. inform and explain). Whichever types of writing you are asked to use, your answer should concentrate on purpose, audience, structure, sentences, vocabulary choice and accuracy.

Revision guide: top 10 tips

1 Draw up a chart (similar to the chart for poem comparison on p. 20) and compare two different non-fiction texts on the same subject. You could look for leaflets in your local library or health centre and then find an article on the same subject on the internet. Alternatively, your English teacher may be able to provide you with some non-fiction material from past exam papers. You should compare:

▶ what the materials are saying
▶ their purpose
▶ their intended audience
▶ use of presentational, organisational and linguistic devices
▶ how well they succeed in their purpose

Remember to look for similarities and differences between the two texts.

2 Use a highlighter pen to pick out the main argument in some front-page stories in a variety of newspapers. Rewrite these main arguments in your

own words. This will prepare you for the Paper 1 question on following an argument and deciding what the writer is talking about.

3 Choose and reread two of the poems from the *Anthology* and compare them using the table on p. 20. Even rereading them without filling in a table will prepare you for the exam, as long as you compare the poems according to the assessment objectives.

4 Work out what each of the poets is saying about different cultures. The poems were chosen for inclusion in the *Anthology* because they have something interesting to say on this subject, whether it is about:
- ▶ their own culture
- ▶ a different culture
- ▶ different views of cultures
- ▶ moving between cultures
- ▶ different cultures in the same country

5 A culture in this context means people's ideas, attitudes, values and beliefs. Ask yourself what some of the poems have to say about these definitions of culture, and compare them with your own cultural background. Can you learn anything new about your own culture, or someone else's, by reading these poems?

6 You must plan your answers if you want to gain the highest marks for writing in Papers 1 and 2. The type of plan you make is individual to you and depends on your learning style, but you must organise your ideas into a sequence. Sequencing will help with the overall structure of your writing and will give you access to a B grade and above. If you think that a paragraph is a mechanical structure approximately eight lines in length, then you are D-grade candidate or below. If, however, you actually understand the job that a paragraph does (which is to help the reader), then you are a B-grade candidate or above.

7 If you are asked to write a letter, article, flier, speech, advice sheet etc., then you should try to make your work look something like those documents by using two or three presentational devices. For example, if you are asked to write an article for a magazine, then a banner headline and some sub-headings would help to make your piece more suited to its purpose, audience and form. However, this is not an art examination, so you should not draw pictures, diagrams, bubble writing etc.

8 Ask your teacher for some past papers and practise writing a response to one of the writing tasks in 45 minutes, using the process outlined on

p. 24. Look back at the assessment objectives for the writing tasks and try to work out how well you have done.

If you have already completed all the past papers available, you can use the two practice questions below to revise for each paper:

Paper 1: Your local council is thinking of banning anyone wearing a hooded top from entering any council building. Write a letter to the council in which you argue for or against this proposal.

Paper 2: Describe your view of the proposal outlined above.

9 Practise writing opening paragraphs for each of the six different types of writing that are examined in Papers 1 and 2. Examiners pay close attention to the beginning of your written piece, so you must make an impact in your opening paragraph. You should:
 ► pay careful attention to purpose and audience
 ► display awareness that you know where your piece is going
 ► use a variety of sentence types
 ► use a wide and sophisticated choice of vocabulary
 ► display some features of the particular type of writing you are using
 ► be accurate

10 The examinations are meant to assess what you can do. You begin each question with no marks and you gain marks for showing evidence of the skills required by the assessment objectives. You should, therefore, revise the assessment objectives covered by each paper.